Pyrrhus Consor, Born Free

by
Joysetta Marsh Pearse

Illustrator
Fatimah T. White

Published by:
TAAGS
P O Box 7385, Freeport NY 11520
ISBN: 0-9792149-3-9
ISBN-13: 978-0-9792149-3-6

DEDICATION

To Sal and Mary St. John, of St. John Productions, who introduced me to the story of Pyrrhus Consor through their theatrical production "Mrs. Gaynor Welcomes Mrs. Pyrrhus Consor" (2002).

CONTENTS

Acknowledgments   i

1   Born Free   Page 1

2   Sailing for Freedom   Page 7

3   After Abolition   Page 9

4   Navigator of the Oceans   Page 17

5   The Gold Rush   Page 19

6   Home and Family   Page 21

7   On Lake Agawam   Page 23

8   In Memoriam   Page 25

ACKNOWLEDGMENTS

Special thanks to Minna Dunn and Vaughn McCall for assisting the research.

1 BORN FREE

Though born free, and legally designated an indentured servant, Pyrrhus Consor was treated as a slave from birth. On March 29, 1799, the New York State Legislature passed "An Act for the Gradual Abolition of Slavery". The Act declared that anyone born of a slave mother after July 4, 1799, was free, with the proviso that said child continue as a servant to the owner of his/her mother until reaching the age of 28, for males, and 25, for females. Pyrrhus was born on March 17, 1814, and was, therefore, legally free; and legally under indenture to Nathan Cooper, the owner of his mother, Violet Williams. (Violet was born 3 Jul 1796[i] and remained enslaved, as the 1799 Act did not apply to her.)

<<   The third entry reads...
1816 Dec 18th
Nathan Cooper Records a Male Child
by the Name Pyrus the Son of Violet a
Slave to me Was born the
17th of March 1814

James Post Town Clerk

The Act further stipulated the responsibilities of the person entitled to the service of the indentured child. According to law, registration of the birth of any free born child was required when the child was nine months old. Registration consisted of delivery of a written certificate (indicating the name of the owner of the indentured child's mother, and the name, age and gender of the child) to the clerk of the municipality in which the owner lived. That certificate was then to be recorded by the clerk in a book provided for that purpose. This registration officially established the child's birth date (and start date of the indenture). The birth date was the determinant of the termination date of the indenture. There was a twelve cents fee to register the certificate and the penalty for not registering within nine months was a fine of five dollars, plus one dollar a month for each month after the child attained nine months and remained unregistered. The income from this process was divided between the clerk's office and funds to be used by the overseers of the poor.

The mother's owner was also responsible for the support of the free-born child. To be relieved of the burden of support, the child could be abandoned to the town's overseers of the poor, at one year old. The child would then be considered a pauper and as such could be bound out by the overseers. Meanwhile New York State covered expenses for the care of the child at three dollars and fifty cents a month.

Nathan Cooper didn't register the birth of "Pyrhus" until December 18, 1816 (*the third entry in the registration pictured on Page 3.*). If he paid the penalty, it would have amounted to thirty-eight dollars. He did not take the abandonment option in 1815, and Cooper died 4 Dec 1817.[ii] Pyrrhus was sold, at five years old (1819), to Elias Pelletreau, a silversmith, born 31 May 1726, in Southampton. (If this was a transfer of the deceased Cooper's right to the child as an indentured servant, it was not so stated. Pyrrhus was sold as if he were a slave.)

This sale occurred despite the New York State Legislature's passing of the 1817 Act Relative to Slaves and Servants. The Act reiterated the servant status of children born to slave mothers as stipulated in the 1799 Act, but added… "every child born of a slave after the passing of this act shall remain a servant as aforesaid until the age of twenty-one years and no longer …every person entitled to the services of any child, under and by virtue of this act, shall, before such child arrive at the age of eighteen years, teach such child, or cause to be taught, to read, so that it may be able to read the holy scriptures, or shall give such child, between the ages of ten and eighteen, four quarters schooling; and if the person so entitled to such service, shall neglect to cause such child to be taught, or to have such schooling, then such child shall be released from its servitude when it shall arrive at the age of eighteen years… *And further*, that in every such case, the overseers of the poor of the city or town in which such child shall or may be or reside, may, and it shall be their duty, forthwith to bind out such child, until it shall have arrived at the age of twenty-one years[iii]".

It has not been determined whether Pyrrhus was purchased by Elias Pelletreau senior or junior, as both had free persons of color and/or slaves within their households between 1790 and 1820. The 1790 United States population census indicates that there was one free person of color and one slave enumerated with Elias senior's family[iv]. Elias junior (born 24 Aug 1757[v]) had just one slave[vi]. Elias senior's other son, John Pelletreau (born 29 Jul 1755) had no free persons of color or slaves in his household.

In 1800, Elias senior was not listed as a head of household, in Southampton. His son, John, however had two adult white males in his household. The male of "up to 45 years of age" was probably himself. The male "of 45 years and up" was probably Elias senior. Again, there were no free persons of color or slaves in John Pelletreau's household.

Elias junior still had one slave, and his neighbor Nathan Cooper listed three[vii]. It cannot be determined from the census data whether Elias Pelletreau junior and Nathan Cooper were in contravention of New York State law, because the identities and ages of the slaves were not noted on the census. If the slaves were born prior to 4 July 1799, they were not freed by the Act for the Gradual Abolition of Slavery of 1799.

The identity of Elias Pelletreau junior's slave hasn't been determined. The evidence suggests that Nathan Cooper's slaves, in 1800, should have been Pyrrhus' mother, Violet, and her parents, Gad and Esther Williams and her sister Rachel. One of the four (probably Rachel at two years old), was not counted in Nathan's household in 1800. Manumission documents show that Nathan Cooper recorded a conditional manumission of Gad and Esther Williams, on 15 Aug 1803[viii]. Their freedom was contingent upon Gad's going on a sea voyage with Captain William Fowler. (As seamen were paid wages, this would afford Cooper income for Gad's service.)

Freedom was not offered to their children in this document. Cooper added that he was reserving his "…right of the male children of the said Esther to serve as the law directs at the age of seven years". Any male sons of Esther's who may have been alive at the time of this manumission have not been identified. The only known son was Prince Gad Williams, who was not born until 3 Jul 1806[ix], and was therefore an indentured servant, at birth.

The conditional manumission made no mention of the daughters of Esther and Gad. Millicent was born 2 Sep1801, also an indentured servant. Violet and Rachel were born in slavery, 3 Jul 1796 and 31 Oct 1798, respectively. Violet has been accounted for in the household of Nathan Cooper[x], but no documentation has been found that establishes the whereabouts of Rachel, in 1800.

Elias Pelletreau senior died 2 Nov 1810[xi]. John, who inherited his father's home, and continued his silversmith business, now had three free persons of color, and no slaves in his household, according to the 1810 census data[xii]. Elias Pelletreau junior had one slave[xiii] and Nathan Cooper's household included four free persons of color, and three slaves[xiv]. Between the households of John and Elias Pelletreau there were three free persons of color and one slave. There is insufficient evidence to make any suggestion as to the identity of the Pelletreau free persons of color or the slave.

Assumptions can be proffered as to the identity of 3 of Nathan's 4 free persons and 2 of the 3 slaves. Gad and Esther were conditionally manumitted in 1803, and are assumed to have been two of the free persons. Their daughter, Millicent, would have been the third free person. Violet (who would become Pyrrhus' mother) and her sister Rachel are assumed to have been two of the three slaves.

2 SAILING FOR FREEDOM

The American Offshore Whaling Voyages database lists several voyages made by Captain William Fowler out of Sag Harbor, between 1804 and 1806. One of which could have been used to fulfill the condition set by Nathan Cooper regarding Gad and Esther Williams' manumission. The first such voyage was aboard the "Minerva", which left in September 1804 for Brazil and returned in June 1805, with 300 pounds of whale.

The next voyage was made in August 1805, aboard the ship "Brazil". It returned from its destination, Patagonia, in July 1806, with a haul of 1,300 pounds of whale. (The master of this ship is simply listed as "Fowler", and could have been William, John or Oliver Fowler, all of whom mastered ships hailing from Sag Harbor within in the same era.)

The third possibility is the voyage of the "Warren" mastered by Captain William Fowler. It left port in August 1806 and returned, from Patagonia, in July 1807, with 1,600 pounds of whale. It is probable that one of the aforesaid voyages had Gad on board. If so, the condition for freedom had been met and although the manumission was not registered until 1811, he and his wife were free in 1810, as per census data.

In 1820, Gad and five other household members were enumerated on the census as free persons of color, under the name "Gadd Cooper". The household were described as: one male under 14 years of age (assumed to be Prince), 1 male 45 and over (assumed to be Gad), two females under 14 (assumed to be Millicent and Rachel, although they were actually 19 and 22), one female of 26 and under 45 (assumed to be Violet, although she was 24), and one female 45 and older (assumed to be Esther at 49).

Nathan Cooper was deceased when the 1820 census was taken. The household of John Pelletreau lists one female free person of color, of 14 and under 26 years old; and one person in the category "All Other Persons except Indians, not taxed" with no age or gender indicated. John's brother Elias (Elias, Junr.) also had one person in the "All Other…" column. The person in John's household was probably Pyrrhus, at six years old. Elias Smith Pelletreau (son of Elias Junr) had become a head of household by 1820, and his household enumeration includes three individuals in the "All Other…" category.

It can't be determined why the census taker noted the record in this way. He/she may have mistakenly marked the wrong column, or perhaps was just unsure of the slave or servant status of the individuals. Mistakes like this have been found in census data from time to time. As with the aforementioned enumeration of Gadd Cooper's family. His 19- and 22-year-old daughters were accounted for in the "under 14" column. They should have been in the next column "14 and under 26". Other sources (baptism records, later census enumerations, etc.) establishes more accurate ages for the family.

Despite its inexactitude in some areas, the 1820 census is a marker on the path toward freedom for the family of Gad Cooper (later known as Gad Williams). They survived the vicissitudes of enslavement; and two documents confirm the release of Gad and Esther, pursuant to Cooper's conditional manumission. On 22 Apr 1811, Nathan Cooper filed a document of manumission for Gad and Esther[xv]. Three years later, on 25 April 1814, Abraham Miller, a Judge of the Court of Common Pleas certified Gad's emancipation[xvi]. (Gad may have applied to the court because he needed documentation that he was free.) Gad was described, as "a black man 46 years old, thick set and about five feet eight inches high".

As Pyrrhus Consor's maternal forbears moved toward freedom, his father, William "Shadrack" Consor, was also freed by his slave owner. In a document dated 8 Jul 1816, Cephas Jagger filed a manumission of "Shadrack"[xvii]. Earlier records indicate that Shadrack had been the slave of William Phillips, who sold him to Joseph Hawkins, on 24 Oct 1798, for eighty pounds[xviii].

3 AFTER ABOLITION

William Shadrach Consor was enumerated in the 1830 census as "Shadrack Will"[xix]. He would have been about 40, and his age classification was "of 36 and under 55". The other household members were: a female who was also "of 36 and under 55"; a female "under 10"; and a female "of ten and under 24". The females were later identified as Shadrach's wife, Armenia, who was about 40, and his daughters Susan and Armenia, who were actually about 6 and 9, respectively.

No male approximating Pyrrhus' age resided with Shadrack Will; but the household of Charles (son of John) Pelletreau included one, male, free person of color. He was of "10 years and under 24"[xx]. Pyrrhus would have been sixteen, and is assumed to be that free person of color.

There were two other free colored families bearing the Consor surname in Southampton in 1830. William Consir (*sic*) headed a household of seven: two males under ten, one male between 11 and 23, one male between 36 and 54, 2 females under 10, and one female between 36 and 54[xxi]. This William was not Pyrrhus' father, Will Shadrach Consor. The two families were distinctly different in composition and were separately enumerated in 1830. They may have been relatives but no documentation has been found that supports kinship.

The other Consor family was headed by John Conser (*sic*), a male "of ten and under 24"[xxii]. His household included one other person, a female "of ten and under 24" subsequently identified as his wife, Philopenia. No evidence of relationship can be determined using this census data, but John's age and consistent proximity to William Shadrach Consor's family over decades, gives rise to an assumption that he was a son, or other relative. He and Philopenia were childless, according to multiple, subsequent census reports.

In 1840, John Consor and William Shadrach Consor were still neighbors. John's household, again, consisted of himself and a female, both in the age bracket 36 and under 55[xxiii]. Shadrach's household consisted of himself at 55 and under 100, a female in the same age bracket (his wife, Armenia) and a female, 10 and under 24 (his daughter Armenia). Susan was probably married by then, and resided with her spouse. There was also a male 10 and under 24. Pyrrhus would have been approximately 26 at the time.

Fortunately, the 1840 census also questioned the industry in which the working household members were involved. Of the two workers, one person (obviously Shadrach) worked in "agriculture", the other person's industry was described as "navigation of the ocean". This was an apt description of Pyrrhus' occupation, as he had been a whaler for eight years, by then. Apparently, Pyrrhus remained in the Charles Pelletreau household through his teen years, and between 1830 and 1840 moved in with his father.

4 NAVIGATOR OF THE OCEANS

During the two decades between 1830 and 1850, Pyrrhus led an adventure-filled life on the sea. At 18, in July 1832, Pyrrhus embarked upon his first sea venture aboard the whaling ship "Boston". He was a "greenie" (a name sea-farers used for a novice) sailing the oceans under Captain Edward D. Sayre. The seven-month whaling voyage from New London, Connecticut to the South Atlantic was successful. The Boston returned, in February 1833, with 1,900 barrels of baleen oil and 16,000 pounds of whale bone[xxiv]. His second voyage was with Captain Jeremiah William Hedges, aboard the "Columbia" (June 1833 – May 1834). The Columbia returned with 75 barrels of oil from sperm whales, 1,685 barrels of baleen[xxv], and 15,000 pounds of whale bone. In the course of his sailing and whaling career Pyrrhus advanced from sailor to sea pilot.

The job of sea pilot on a whaling ship required both great courage and skill. Taking down the whale required spearing it with a harpoon that was tethered to the whale boat. After the whale was harpooned, the pilot had to steer a dangerous course to avoid capsizing. The whale, flailing to get free, could create a life-threatening situation.

Pyrrhus was lauded as an excellent steersman, and was chosen by Captain Mercator Cooper, son of Nathan Cooper, to pilot the "Manhattan" on an unexpectedly historic journey. It was a whaling expedition that brought them to the port at Yeddo (now Tokyo), Japan, and into the annals of maritime history.

On November 9, 1843, Captain Cooper, pilot Pyrrhus Consor and the crew sailed out of Southampton aboard the Manhattan[xxvi]. They were sailing in the North Pacific, in April 1846, when they came upon eleven ship-wrecked Japanese sailors on an island in the Bonin archipelago, called St. Peters Island.[xxvii] They took the men on board and planned to take them to the port at Yeddo. They not only encountered severe storms, but came across another crew of eleven shipwrecked Japanese sailors and took them aboard also. Captain Cooper was determined to return the men to their homeland, but thought it prudent to dispatch four of the rescued sailors to advise the Japanese officials of his imminent arrival[xxviii]. There was apprehension that an unannounced visit might create problems since Japan was a country in seclusion and foreign occidental vessels were not allowed to enter her ports.

For reasons both political and religious, a series of edicts had been issued by Japanese shoguns from 1623 to 1651, with the intent of creating seclusion for Japan. The most effective of the series was the Sakoku Edict of 1635. It banned Catholic missionaries; led to the expulsion of the Portuguese in 1639; and eventually closed Japan to most of the western world. There was an exception, however. The port of Nagasaki was allowed to conduct limited trade with Holland's Dutch East India Company[xxix]. When the Manhattan entered the bay at Yeddo, it was met by close to three hundred Japanese boats, each carrying about fifteen men, armed with spears, swords and knives.

Captain Cooper and crew were not permitted to disembark. A party of Japanese dignitaries boarded the Manhattan and, although the Japanese were wary of the other crewmen, they were fascinated by Pyrrhus, Gad Williams and a Native American named Eleazar. [Note] *The "Gad Williams" referred to here is Prince Gad Williams, Pyrrhus' uncle. His grandfather, Gad Williams, died between August and October 1841.*[xxx] Accounts of the initial sighting of Pyrrhus by the Japanese have indicated that the Japanese were astounded by his dark complexion. This cannot be so, as the Japanese were well-acquainted with dark-skinned people. Also, Pyrrhus' physical resemblance to the aboriginal people of Hokkaido may have triggered the Japanese sense of awe.

Ainu Man

Council of the Elders

Indigenous Ainu Conduct a Bear Ceremony

These are but a few reasons why it is incorrect to state or imply that Japanese were unfamiliar with people of Pyrrhus' complexion.

Additionally, the Black shogun, Sakanouye no Tamura Maro was one of the most honored and respected militarists in early Japan. Occidental historians have described him as a Negro. He was, however, descended from China's Emperor Ling. Tamura Maro was a fierce warrior, and a paragon of military virtue and prowess during the reign of the Japanese Emperor Kwammu (782 - 806 A.D.).

Japan conducted trade with East Asians and Africans throughout the two centuries of isolation from the west. The Mongols, a people of various shades of yellow, brown and black, were fierce enemies of Japan. Their leader, Kublai Khan, made several unsuccessful attempts to defeat her in the 13th century.

The following drawing of the 1853 visit of Commodore Perry to Japan depicts Japanese of various complexions, the guardsman in the foreground being the darkest.

Commodore Perry's Arrival for a Meeting with Japanese Dignitaries (1853)

Pyrrhus was possessed of a great singing voice and sang when they gathered socially. That, and his lauded demeanor may have contributed to their admiration of him.

After four days, the Manhattan prepared to depart. The Japanese provided staples for the journey (rice, wheat, flour, tobacco, sweet potatoes, radishes, fowl, supplies and delicacies). Captain Cooper also managed to obtain a map of Japan. Upon the departure of the Manhattan, Cooper was given a stern warning against ever returning.[xxxi] Captain Cooper shared the map's data with American authorities. That information is said to have been used by Commodore Matthew C. Perry, who is credited with opening Japan to western trade. The original map was eventually donated to the New Bedford Whaling Museum in Massachusetts, by Mercator's descendants.

Other commentaries on this event assert that the Manhattan's peaceful venture into Japanese waters paved the way for Perry. Based upon events that occurred after the Manhattan's departure, it's not very likely that one event influenced the other.

In September 1846, the ship, Lawrence, was lost off the coast of Japan and (of the entire crew) only the second mate and seven seamen reached the shore alive. They were immediately seized by the Japanese and imprisoned for seventeen months, during which they were insulted and beaten. One sailor, who attempted escape, was summarily executed[xxxii].

Similar to the experience of the Lawrence was that of the Lagoda, of New Bedford, also wrecked on a Japanese island. Those of the crew who survived the wreck were so inhumanely treated, that one of their number committed suicide[xxxiii].

Far from a peaceful approach, on July 8, 1853, Commodore Perry entered the Port at Yeddo with a fleet of four warships on July 8, 1853. The Japanese fleet, although officially hostile, was unable to match the potential force of American warships. On a mission to initiate diplomatic and trade agreements with Japan, Perry used threats of attack to intimidate, and succeeded in opening negotiations. He carried with him a letter from President Millard Fillmore that proposed peace and amity; and he left with a commitment to friendship between the two nations.

The following year, the Commodore returned to Japan and negotiated a treaty of peace, friendship and trade, dated March 31, 1854. This was a major accomplishment for Perry; and it signaled Japan's re-entry to world trade.

The 1854 treaty was a boon to both nations: the United States winning commercial access, protection for its citizens and opportunity for exchange of ideas; and Japan entering upon its modern era, using concepts and knowledge from the west; and emerging as a great industrial country and a formidable military power.

5 THE GOLD RUSH

Before his Japanese adventure, in 1843, Pyrrhus' widowed grandmother, Esther, granted him her house and property due to her inability to handle her affairs[xxxiv]. The land deeded was described as two acres, bound on the North by land of Pyrrhus; East by the road and partly by land of her son, Prince Williams; South partly by Prince Williams and partly by Barry Green; and West by Schuyler B. Halsey[xxxv].

Pyrrhus' life on the ocean apparently provided an income sufficient to acquire property, marry, and start a family. No record of his marriage has been located but it probably occurred around 1847, after his return from Japan. Although married and a land-owner, Pyrrhus was still attracted to adventure. When the California "gold rush" began, he was among the "forty-niners".

For the purpose of heading for the gold mines and possibly making a fortune, a group of eastern Long Islanders formed a corporation, the "Southampton and California Mining and Trading Company". They set sail for San Francisco, California on 8 February 1848, aboard the ship "The Sabina". The company's 60 share-holders (15 of whom were Captains) were: Capt. Henry Green (Trustee, Treasurer and President), Capt. James Parker (Trustee), Capt. Barney R Green (Trustee), Capt. Laufaette Ludlow (Trustee), Albert Jagger (Trustee), Capt. Albert Rogers Trustee), A. J. Tabor (Trustee & Secretary), Capt. David Hand, Capt. Edward W Halsey, Capt. Schuyler B. Halsey, Capt. Charles Howel, Capt. John Woodward, Capt. William C Hanes, Capt. Joseph Case, Capt. Doyl Sweeney, Capt. William Post, Edward White, David H. Hand, Jetur Reeves, John Van Vechten, Edwin Isham, George Herrick (substitute for James Herrick), Daniel Glover, John H Green, Charles N. Green, William W. Tinker, Capt. William S Denison (Sold out to George Post) Thomas W. Warren, Andrew L. Edwards (substitute for B.C. Payne), David F Parker (Substitute for William Adams), James Mc Cue, John Cook (Substitute for John Bishop Jr.), George H. Burnett, William Halsey, Spencer F. Sayre (for Isaac Sayre Jr.), William White, Henry Rhodes, Thomas Glover (Substitute for G. S. Adams), Albert Hildreth, Samuel B. Halsey, William F. Horton), Isaac Van Scoy, William H.

Post, William M. Parker (Substitute for James M. Godbee), Thomas P. Ripley (Substitute for G. S. Adams), Jonathan K. Fields, Salter S. Horton, Thomas L Mc Elrath, Lewis Jagger, Austin Jagger, Peter H. Howell, Augustus Ludlow (Substitute for Nathan Y. Fordham), Nathan Dimond, Jedediah Conklin, Doct. (*sic*), John L. Dodge, Lewis Sandford, James Rogers (Substitute for Barney R. Green), Henry Webb, Alfred H. Sandford and John Crook (Substitute for Charles W. Payne). After the first 60 shares were distributed, four more shares were issued to H. Green (3 shares) and to Capt D. Hand (1 share).[xxxvi]

Eight passengers paid one hundred and fifty dollars passage. They were C.W. Hatch, Charles N. Howell, George Howell, John R. Miller, Horatio Rogers, Noel Byron Rogers, Charles Sealy and Theodore J. Wood. A cook, Alfonzo Boardman, two stewards, John Hull and Job Heages worked for their passage, as did fifteen seaman. The fifteen were Watson Coney, Erastus Glover, Smith Bellows, Poyrres[?] Conce (*sic*), Daniel Howell, Napoleon Griffing, Absolom Griffing, Nathan Post, Franklin C. Jessup, Stephen French, Robert Gavainen, Wm F Huntting, George Post, Charles Crook and John Killis.[xxxvii] Pyrrhus and six other working seaman were also half-share holders.[xxxviii]

The Sabina left Long Island from Greenport[xxxix] and once at sea, proved to be less than seaworthy. The crew spent most of the first two weeks at the pumps, trying to stay afloat. The navigator, Henry Green, kept a journal and the 86-page document reveals much of the activities on board, and the events that occurred in California.

Green describes the tumultuous journey, sailing around Cape Horne to reach their destination. It was a voyage fraught with rough seas, gales and the effects of a faltering ship. The Sabina finally dropped anchor far inside the Bay of San Francisco, miles from the city of the same name. The port of arrival was off the city of Pittsburg, California (named for Pittsburgh Pennsylvania). They arrived on 12 August 1849.

The company started to disintegrate soon after the men purchased their gear, set up camp, and commenced their search for gold. The prospectors found little gold, but many who had some success, decided not to honor their agreement to share. Of the fifteen seamen who worked for their passage, only seven remained with what was left of the company members. The seamen who stayed were Franklin C Jessup, Watson Coney[?], Poyrres Conce (*sic*), Daniel Howell, Nathan Post, Charles Crook, John Killis, and George Post.[xl] The group prospected, but no significant find was made. Sickness and death took their toll, and the search was abandoned.

Less than nine months after their arrival, the Sabina, manned by a skeleton crew that included Pyrrhus, was sailed back to the City of San Francisco so she could be sold to the highest bidder. The last leg of Pyrrhus' journey back home is documented on the Passenger List of Vessels Arriving in New York. He boarded the ship " Georgia" and departed from Chagres, Panama via Havana, Cuba and arrived in New York on 7 Dec 1850[xli]. He was described as a mechanic, and probably worked for his passage on this ship also.

6 HOME AND FAMILY

The census of 1850 was the first US population enumeration to list each member of every household, by name. Pyrrhus, at 36, was head of a household that included Rachel Consor (44), James Harvey Consor (2) and Esther Williams (79)[xlii]. Later documentation identified Rachel as his wife, and James Harvey as his son. All of the adults in the household were literate, and all members were born in New York. Pyrrhus' occupation was "seaman".

Pyrrhus' grandmother Esther, having turned her house and property over to him in 1843, was included in his 1850 household. It is not clear whether he moved his family into her home, or brought Esther into his.

Pyrrhus and Rachel had one other male child, Charles Consor, who died in infancy. Oddly, Southampton Town Records indicate two male children (obviously twins) were born to "Pyrhus and Esther Gad" on 20 Aug 1847. The date approximates the year of birth for James Harvey calculated as 1848, based on 1850 and 1860 census reports. Esther The parents' names should have been indicated as Pyrrhus and Rachel Consor.

This instance of error is one of many, official and unofficial misspellings of Pyrrhus' name, or use of a wrong surname. In the 1843 deed between Pyrrhus and Esther he is named Pyrrhus Gad. The spelling of his surname was Consor on census data until 1870, when it was listed as Concer. His death certificate and grave marker both use the latter spelling, but his death certificate differs from the grave marker as it relates to his date of birth. The death certificate states April 18, 1814[xliii], and the grave marker (and his birth registration) indicate March 17, 1814. Most references to him in ship logs have egregious errors in spelling both given and surnames.

In 1850, Pyrrhus' uncle, Prince, still maintained his home and property next door, and was described as a 44 year-old laborer. Mary Williams was 47, and Harriet Williams was 15.[xliv] Mary and Harriet later proved to be his wife and daughter.

8 IN MEMORIAM

Pyrrhus Consor died, of natural cause, on 23 August 1897. His official death certificate places his death at Southampton Hospital, 240 Meeting House Lane, Southampton, New York. This appears to be in error, since the Southampton Hospital Foundation was established in 1909, by New York City physician, Dr. Albert Ely and others. The hospital didn't open until 1913. Pyrrhus' death certificate also incorrectly cites William Moore as his father, not William Shadrach Consor.

Pyrrhus' mother, Violet, married William M. Moore, after leaving Southampton as a young woman. (Violet and William resided New York City,[lviii] and are presumed to have died there.) Pyrrhus is buried at the old North End Cemetery, in Southampton.

He had gained much popularity, and his death was widely reported. His Last Will and Testament attracted a great deal of press also. Several charitable and religious organizations (e.g.) the American Seaman's Friend Society, and the Presbyterian Church of Southampton, were bequeathed portions of his monetary estate.

There were no bequests for relatives, several of whom, jointly, initiated a suit to contest the will. When the hearing was held before Surrogate Judge Nathan D. Petty, the executor, Henry H. Hildreth stated that he spoke with Pyrrhus regarding the exclusion of relatives, and asked if he had considered including them. Pyrrhus responded, "No, not one cent. Let them scratch as I have had to".[lix] The will was ruled to be valid, and was probated on 23 April 1898.

In the Old North End Cemetery, in Southampton, a marker was placed on the grave where Pyrrhus and Rachel were buried. The epitaph reflects the high esteem and affection his neighbor, Salem Wales, had for Pyrrhus, although the slave reference is incorrect.

THOUGH BORN A SLAVE
HE POSSESSED THOSE
VIRTUES, WITHOUT WHICH,
KINGS ARE BUT SLAVES.

ADDENDUM

<u>Kinship Report of Pyrrhus Consor</u>

Name:	**Birth Date:**	**Relationship:**
Adams, Alfred	Jan 1870	1st cousin 1x removed
Adams, Alfred Jr.	1908	1st cousin 2x removed
Adams, Lena Sp-Alfred Jr.	1908	Wife of 1st cousin 1x removed
Adams, Louisa M.	Nov 1862	1st cousin 1x removed
Adams, Margaret	1905	1st cousin 2x removed
Adams, Mary	Jan 1896	1st cousin 2x removed
Adams, Pauline	About 1902	1st cousin 2x removed
Adams, Pearl	About 1910	1st cousin 2x removed
Adams, Ralph	1919	1st cousin 2x removed
Adams, Raymond	1916	1st cousin 2x removed
Adams, Ruby E.	About 1900	1st cousin 2x removed
Adams, Sarah	Aug 1863	1st cousin 1x removed
Adams, William	About 1826	Husband of 1st cousin
Adams, William Jr.	About 1858	1st cousin1x removed
Anderson, Bruce	May 1898	Bro-in-law of nephew of husband of 1st cousin1x removed
Anderson, Cornelia O.	Aug 1884	Sis-in-law of nephew of husband of 1st cousin1x removed
Anderson, Douglas	Oct 1894	Bro-in-law of nephew of husband of 1st cousin1x removed
Anderson, Edwin P.	Jun 1887	Bro-in-law of nephew of husband of 1st cousin1x removed
Anderson, Gilbert	1906	Bro-in-law of nephew of husband of 1st cousin1x removed
Anderson, Hazel	1903	Sis-in-law of nephew of husband of 1st cousin1x removed

Name:	Birth Date:	Relationship:
Anderson, James	About 1830	Husband of 1st cousin
Anderson, Kate Margarite	Jan 1891	Sis-in-law of nephew of husband of 1st cousin 1x removed
Anderson, Mildred	1901	Sis-in-law of nephew of husband of 1st cousin 1x removed
Anderson, Robert F.	Sep 1856	Father-in-law of nephew of husband of 1st cousin 1x removed
Anderson, Robt. F. Jr.	Jul 1882	Bro-in-law of nephew of husband of 1st cousin 1x removed
Anderson, Vernon E.	Mar 1889	Bro-in-law of nephew of husband of 1st cousin 1x removed
Anderson, Wesley	About 1912	Husband of 1st cousin 3x removed
Arch, James	Oct 1805	Husband of aunt
Arch, Samuel	1831	Maternal 1st cousin
Ashman, Alberta Dolores	1909	1st cousin 3x removed
Ashman, Alice	1918	1st cousin 3x removed
Ashman, Arthur	1884	Husband of 1st cousin 2x removed
Ashman, Charles	1856	Uncle of husband of 1st cousin 2x removed
Ashman, Charles	1916	1st cousin 3x removed
Ashman, Grant	1918	1st cousin 3x removed
Ashman, Helen	Private	1st cousin 3x removed
Ashman, Maria Geneva	1858	Mother-in-law of 1st cousin 2x removed
Ashman, Marion	Private	1st cousin 3x removed
Ashman, Mary Helen	1885	1st cousin of husband of 1st cousin 2x removed
Ashman, Miles	1825	Maternal grandfather of husband of 1st cousin 2x removed

Name:	Birth Date:	Relationship:
Ashman, Sarah II	1914	1st cousin 3x removed
Ashman, Talullah	1912	1st cousin 3x removed
Brinette, Lucinda	1800	Great grandmother of 1st cousin 2x removed
Brown, Elmer	About 1895	Husband of sis-in-law of nephew of husband of 1st cousin 1x removed
Brown, Philip III	Private	Husband of 1st cousin 3x removed
Certain, Bisby Wilhelm	1916	Nephew of husband of 1st cousin 2x removed
Certain, Charles C.	Private	Nephew of husband of 1st cousin 2x removed
Certain, Elmer	1888	Husband of sis-in-law of 1st cousin 2x removed
Certain, Horatio Bisby	1883	Husband of sis-in-law of 1st cousin 2x removed
Certain, Noal	1918	Nephew of husband of 1st cousin 2x removed
Certain, Rodney Q.	1914	Nephew of husband of 1st cousin 2x removed
Consor, Armenia	1825	Half sister
Consor, Armenia Sp2- of Wm. Shadrach	1800	Stepmother
Consor, Charles	About 1848	Son
Consor, James Harvey	About 1848	Son
Consor, Pyrrhus	17 Mar 1814	Self
Consor, William Shadrach	1790	Father
Crippen, Alfred A.	1916	1st cousin 3x removed
Crippen, Anita L.	1908	1st cousin 3x removed
Crippen, Arthur Jr.	Private	1st cousin 4x removed
Crippen, Arthur L.	1908	1st cousin 3x removed
Crippen, Bertha Elisabeth	1889	Sis-in-law of 1st cousin 2x removed
Crippen, Carmen	Private	1st cousin 4x removed
Crippen, Charles	1876	Bro-in-law of 1st cousin 2x removed

Name:	Birth Date:	Relationship:
Crippen, Earl F.	1918	1st cousin 3x removed
Crippen, Edward L.	1913	1st cousin 3x removed
Crippen, Emmett Arthur	12 Apr 1883	Husband of 1st cousin 2x removed
Crippen, Florence	1878	Sis-in-law of 1st cousin 2x removed
Crippen, Florence J.	06/Oct 1924	1st cousin 3x removed
Crippen, Frank A.	1919	1st cousin 3x removed
Crippen, Harriett R.	Private	1st cousin 3x removed
Crippen, Helen	1886	Sis-in-law of 1st cousin 2x removed
Crippen, Jean	Private	1st cousin 4x removed
Crippen, Lawrence E.	Private	1st cousin 3x removed
Crippen, Mary A.	1914	1st cousin 3x removed
Crippen, Maud	Nov 1879	Sis-in-law of 1st cousin 2x removed
Crippen, Roma	Private	1st cousin 4x removed
Crippen, Thomas	Private	1st cousin 4x removed
Crippen, Wayne	Private	1st cousin 4x removed
Crippen, William E.	Jan 1846	Father-in-law of 1st cousin 2x removed
Cuffee Frances	1851	Wife of uncle of husband of 1st cousin 2x removed
Cuffee, Helen	1835	Maternal grandmother of husband of 1st cousin 2x removed
Cuffee, Sp-Armenia Consor	About 1820	Husband of half sister
Cuzzens, Earl A.	Dec 1899	Nephew of husband of 1st cousin 1x removed
Cuzzens, Eleanor	Nov 1895	Niece of husband of 1st cousin 1x removed
Cuzzens, George L.	Feb 1861	Husband of sis-in-law of 1st cousin 1x removed
Cuzzens, George L. Jr	Jul 1899	Nephew of husband of 1st cousin 1x removed

Name:	Birth Date:	Relationship:
Cuzzens, Inez Gomez	27 Jul 1897	Grand niece of husband of 1st cousin 1x removed
Cuzzens, Lorena M.	July 1897	Niece of husband of 1st cousin 1x removed
Cuzzens, Lowell H.	Oct 1863	Nephew of husband of 1st cousin 1x removed
Cuzzens, Sivana A.	1904	Niece of husband of 1st cousin 1x removed
Davis, Anna H.	Dec 1890	Sis-in-law of 1st cousin 2x removed
Davis, Arthur P. Jr	Private	1st cousin 3x removed
Davis, Arthur Poland	23 Feb 1894	Husband of 1st cousin 2x removed
Davis, Bernard	Dec 1881	Bro-in-law of 1st cousin 2x removed
Davis, Bernard II	Private	1st cousin 3x removed
Davis, Bette A.	Private	1st cousin 3x removed
Davis, Edward H.	Aug 1886	Bro-in-law of 1st cousin 2x removed
Davis, Hannibal L.	Apr 1898	Bro-in-law of 1st cousin 2x removed
Davis, Ida W. Sp-Wm	Mar 1862	Mother-in-law of 1st cousin 2x removed
Davis, Lester A.	Private	1st cousin 3x removed
Davis, Mary E.	Private	1st cousin 3x removed
Davis, Sophia	Dec 1884	Sis-in-law of 1st cousin 2x removed
Davis, William H. Jr	Aug 1888	Bro-in-law of 1st cousin 2x removed
Davis, William H.	May 1860	Father-in-law of 1st cousin 2x removed
Franklin, Edgar	1905	1st cousin 3x removed
Franklin, Eleanor H.	Private	1st cousin 4x removed
Franklin, Elizabeth	1903	1st cousin 3x removed
Franklin, Elizabeth	1907	1st cousin 3x removed
Franklin, Sp-Florence Lee	about 1880	Husband of 1st cousin 2x removed

Name:	Birth Date:	Relationship:
Green, Elizabeth	1885	Mother-in-law of grand niece of husband of 1st cousin 1x removed
Gumbs, Lance	Private	1st cousin 4x removed
Gumbs, Lancelot	Private	Husband of 1st cousin 3x removed
Harris, Daisy		Wife of 1st cousin 2x removed
Hatcher, Elizabeth	1878	Wife of Father-in-law of grand niece of husband of 1st cousin 1x removed
Hearn, Rodney	Private	1st cousin 4x removed
Hearn, Sp-Anita Crippen		Husband of 1st cousin 3x removed
Hunter, Beulah	1896	Stepdaughter of mother-in-law of of 1st cousin 2x removed
Hunter, Pearl	1900	Stepdaughter of mother-in-law of 1st cousin 2x removed
Hunter, Wiley	1865	Husband of mother-in-law of 1st cousin 2x removed
Jackson, Jacob	About 1800	Husband of aunt
Jackson, Harriet E.	1858	Mother-in-law of 1st cousin of husband of 1st cousin 2x removed
Jenkins, Sp-Sophia Davis	About 1880	Husband of sis-in-law of 1st cousin 2x removed
Johnson, Sp-Della Lee	About 1880	Husband of 1st cousin 2x removed
Johnson, William	May 1857	Husband of sis-in-law of 1st cousin 1x removed
Joseph, Maria	About 1850	Paternal grandmother of husband of grand niece of 1st cousin 1x removed

Name:	Birth Date:	Relationship:
Kellis, Blanche E.	1916	Niece of husband of 1st cousin of 1st cousin 2x removed
Kellis, David	1866	Father-in-law of 1st cousin of husband of 1st cousin 2x removed
Kellis, David Elwood	03 Aug 1885	Brother-in-law of 1st cousin of husband of 1st cousin 2x removed
Kellis, David Elwood Jr	1914	Nephew of husband of 1st cousin of husband of 1st cousin 2x removed
Kellis, Elsie L.	1913	Niece of husband of 1st cousin of husband of 1st cousin 2x removed
Kellis, Estelle	1885	Sis-in-law of 1st cousin of husband of 1st cousin 2x removed
Kellis, Eva H.	Private	Niece of husband of 1st cousin of husband of 1st cousin 2x removed
Kellis, George T.	1888	Brother-in-law of 1st cousin of husband of 1st cousin 2x removed
Kellis, Isabelle	1885	Sis-in-law of 1st cousin of husband of 1st cousin 2x removed
Kellis, James L.	Private	Nephew of husband of 1st cousin of husband of 1st cousin 2x removed
Kellis, John C.	Private	1st cousin 1x removed of husband of 1st cousin 2x removed
Kellis, Marguerite Sp- David Elwood	1894	Wife of brother-in-law of 1st cousin of husband of 1st cousin 2x removed

Name:	Birth Date:	Relationship:
Kellis, Pearl M.	Private	Niece of husband of 1st cousin of husband of 1st cousin 2x removed
Kellis, Percy Claybourn	1882	Husband of 1st cousin of husband of 1st cousin 2x removed
Kellis, Winifred	Private	Niece of husband of 1st cousin of husband of 1st cousin 2x removed
Lee, Agnes dau.-Vera M .	Private	1st cousin 4x removed
Lee, Agnes C. Sp1-Ferdinand	Oct 1885	Wife of 1st cousin 2x rem'd.
Lee, Alice	1918	1st cousin 3x removed
Lee, Clara	Private	1st cousin 3x removed
Lee, Della	May 1885	1st cousin 2x removed
Lee, Everett	Sep 1861	Husband of 1st cousin 1x removed
Lee, Everett Belmont	Jan 1892	1st cousin 2x removed
Lee, Ferdinand	12 Aug 1887	1st cousin 2x removed
Lee, Florence	Jul 1881	1st cousin 2x removed
Lee, Harriett A.	Nov 1889	1st cousin 2x removed
Lee, Idella	Private	1st cousin 3x removed
Lee, James	Private	1st cousin 4x removed
Lee, Mary E.	Nov 1893	1st cousin 2x removed
Lee, Robert	Jun 1882	1st cousin 2x removed
Lee, Vera M.	03 Sep 1911	1st cousin 3x removed
Lee, William B.	26 Oct 1907	1st cousin 3x removed
Lynch, Rosemary	1918	Niece of husband of 1st cousin 2x removed
Lynch, Sp-AnnaDavis	About 1890	Husband of sis-in-law of cousin 1x removed
McClane, Curtis B.	1918	Nephew of the wife of nephew of husband of 1st cousin 1x removed
McClane, Kenneth	1914	Nephew of the wife of nephew of husband of 1st cousin 1x removed

Name:	Birth Date:	Relationship:
McClane, Walter Dorey	About 1880	Husband of sis-in-law of nephew of husband of 1st cousin 1x removed
McClane, Walter Dorey Jr	1911	Nephew of the wife of nephew of husband of 1st cousin 1x removed
Moore, William M.	1800	Stepfather
Morrell, Frank	1900	Husband of 1st cousin 2x rem'd.
Morrell, Frank Jr	Private	1st cousin 3x removed
Morrell, Joseph	Private	1st cousin 3x removed
Morrell, Marjorie	Private	1st cousin 3x removed
Ryer, Addison J.	1820	Father-in-law of 1st cousin 1x removed
Ryer, Addison J. II	1897	1st cousin 2x removed
Ryer, Augusta	Aug 1853	Sis-in-law of 1st cousin 1x rem'd.
Ryer, Augusta M.	1883	1st cousin 2x removed
Ryer, Freelove	Jun 1858	Bro-in-law of 1st cousin 1x removed
Ryer, Inez V.	1896	1st cousin 2x removed
Ryer, Jesse	1862	Bro-in-law of 1st cousin 1x removed
Ryer, Lorena	1867	Sis-in-law of 1st cousin 1x rem'd.
Ryer, Marion L.	May 1867	Sis-in-law of 1st cousin 1x rem'd.
Ryer, Nancy J. Sp-Addison	1824	Mother-in-law of 1st cousin 1x removed
Ryer, Ulysses Grant	Jun 1865	Husband of 1st cousin 1x rem.
Schomburg, Arthur Alfonso	24 Jan 1874	Father-in-law of grand niece of husband of 1st cousin 1x removed
Schomburg, Arthur Alfonso Jr		Half-bro of husband of grand niece of husband of 1st cousin cousin 1x removed
Schomburg, Carlos Federico	About 1840	Paternal grandfather of hus-band of grand niece of hus-

band of 1st cousin 1x rem'd.

Name:	Birth Date:	Relationship:
Schomburg, Carlos Placido	1917	Bro-in-law of grand niece of husband of 1st cousin 1x removed
Schomburg, Dolores Maria	1915	Sis-in-law of grand niece of husband of 1st cousin1x removed
Schomburg, Fernando Alfonso	Aug 1912	Husband of grand niece of husband of 1st cousin 1x removed
Schomburg, Kingsley Guarionex	May 1900	Half-bro of husband of grand niece of husband of 1st cousin1x removed
Schomburg, Maximo Gomez	1909	Half-bro of husband of grand niece of husband of 1st cousin1x removed
Schomburg, Nathaniel Jose	1909	Half-bro of husband of grand niece of husband of 1st cousin1x removed
Schomburg, Reginald Stanton	Private	Half-bro of husband of grand niece of husband of 1st cousin1x removed
Taylor, Elizabeth Morrow	About 1891	Wife of Father-in-law of grand niece of husband of husband of 1st cousin 1x removed
Thomas, Jacob	1854	Husband of sis-in-law of 1st cousin 1x removed
Thomas, unnamed	Apr 1900	Niece of husband of 1st cousin 1x removed
Thomas, Vida M.	Jan 1898	Niece of husband of 1st cousin 1x removed
Turner, Anilda	1912	Wife of 1st cousin 3x removed
Williams, Aaron	1816	Bro-in-law

Williams, Abraham	1832	Bro-in-law
Williams, Esther Sp-Gad	1771	Maternal grandmother
Williams, Elizabeth	08 Aug 1835	Maternal 1st cousin
Williams, Gad Cooper	1768	Maternal grandfather
Williams, Harriet Ann	29 Nov 1836	Maternal 1st cousin
Williams, Jeptha	1774	Father-in-law
Williams, John	1824	Bro-in-law
Williams, Mary E. Sp-Prince	1803	Wife of uncle
Williams, Millicent	02 Sep 1801	Aunt
Williams, Nancy Sp-Jeptha	1782	Mother-in-law
Williams, Prince Gad	03 Jul 1806	Uncle
Williams, Rachel	31 Oct 1798	Aunt
Williams, Rachel A.	Mar 1806	Wife
Williams, Violet	03 Jul 1796	Mother
Williams, William Francis	1839	Maternal 1st cousin

NOTE: Dates of birth for persons born after 1919 are "Private".

A full genealogy for Pyrrhus Consor may be accessed at www.ancestry.com. It is posted in "Family Trees", as **Consor 2014-04-15**.

About the Author

Joysetta Marsh Pearse, was born in Brooklyn, New York and attended schools in Bedford-Stuyvesant, Brownsville and Crown Heights (Holy Rosary, P.S. 175, Glenmore J.H.S. and Bishop McDonnell Memorial High School).

A graduate of Nassau Community College (A.A degree) and Adelphi University (B.A. degree) she retired from NYNEX Corporation in 1990 and has devoted most of her retirement years to genealogical and historical research. With her husband, Julius, she co-founded The African Atlantic Genealogical Society in 1994.

Joysetta, a MENSAN, was certified by the Board for Certification of Genealogists, in 2005; and has served six years as President of the Genealogy Federation of Long Island. Since February, 2012 Joysetta and Julius have managed operations and programs at the African American Museum of Nassau County, in Hempstead, New York.

Her books reflect years of historical and genealogical research and are extensions of the "hidden history" exhibits she develops for the museum. The first book in her Black Royals series("Black Royals: Queen Charlotte") was published in January 2014, and publications in progress are "Black Royals: Queen Philippa" (August 2014) and "Black Royals: Queen Yaa Asantewaa" (December 2014).

[i] *Births and Baptisms*, Presbyterian Church of Southampton, comp. by Daughters of the American Revolution, Southampton Colony Chapter, p.10.

[ii] www.FindAGrave.com; Grave marker , in Southampton Cemetery, Suffolk County, New York, Find a Grave memorial # 22319531

[iii] An Act for the Gradual Abolition of Slavery, passed by the New York State Legislature, 29 March 1799, articles I and V, copy in possession of writer.

[iv] US population census 1790, New York, Suffolk Co., South Hampton, NARA Schedule: M637-6, p.166, sh.132, l.33, Household of Elias "Pellatreau".

[v] *The Pelletreau Family Papers*, ARC 142, Box 3 of 3 (filed in Alpha order), Brooklyn Historical Society, 128 Pierrepont Street, Brooklyn NY 11201

[vi] Ibid. p.167, sh.133, l.13, Household of Elias "Pellatreau" Jun[r].

[vii] US population census 1800, New York, Suffolk Co., South Hampton, NARA Schedule: M32-27, p.97, l.6, Household of John "Peltreau"; l.11, Household of Nathan Cooper; and l.15, Household of Elias "Peltreau" Jun[r].

[viii] *The Fourth Book of Records of the Town of Southampton, Long Island, N.Y.*, Sag Harbor, John H. Hunt, Printer, 1896, p.6.

[ix] See *supra* note i.

[x] See *supra* note vii, p. 30/25, birth registration for "Pyrus, son of Violet"

[xi] See *supra* note iv.

[xii] US population census 1810, New York, Suffolk Co., South Hampton, NARA Schedule: M252-36, p.206, l.23, Household of John Pelletreau.

[xiii] Ibid. p.207, l.23, Household of Elias Pelletreau [no longer listed as "Junr"].

[xiv] US population census 1810, New York, Suffolk Co., South Hampton, NARA Schedule: M252-36, p.207, l.3, Household of Nathan Cooper.

[xv] See *supra*, note vii, p.6/18

[xvi] See *supra*, note vii, p.18/28

[xvii] See *supra*, note vii, p.28/40

[xviii] *Bill of Sale: William Phillips to Joseph Hawkins*, sale of Shadrack. Pennypacker Long Island Collection, Repository, East Hampton Library, East Hampton, New York

[xix] United States Population Census 1830, New York, Suffolk County,

Southampton Town, NARA Schedule M19-103, p. 232, l.11, Household of "Shadrack Will".

xx Ibid. p.226, l.26, Household of Charles Pelletreau

xxi United States Population Census 1830, New York, Suffolk County, Southampton Town, NARA Schedule M19-103, p. 215, l.15, Household of William "Consir"

xxii Ibid. p.232, l.13, Household of John Conser *(sic)*.

xxiii United States Population Census 1840, New York, Suffolk County, Southampton Town, p. 151, l.25, Household of John Consor.

xxiv National Maritime Digital Library, American Offshore Whaling Voyages: A Database, (Indexed alphabetically by vessel name), www.nmdl.org

xxv Baleen is stiff matter from baleen whale jaws that filters tiny pieces of food entering the mouth from the ocean. It was used for corseting, umbrella ribs, etc.

xxvi OCLC World Catalog database. www.worldcat.org

xxvii United States Naval Institute Proceedings, Volume 31, Issue 2, p.952, Publisher: The Institute, Annapolis, Maryland, 1905.

xxviii See vi, supra.

xxix Deal, William E., Handbook to Life in Medieval and Early Modern Japan, p.127, Publisher: Oxford University Press, 2005

xxx Proving of the Last Will and Testament of Gad Williams, at Surrogate's Court held at the house of John White, in Southampton, Suffolk County, New York, before Surrogate Judge George Miller, witnessed by Mehitabel and Silvanus S. White, on 1 Nov 1841. Copy in possession of Writer.

xxxi *Transactions of the Albany Institute*, by Albany Institute, vol. 9, p.151.

xxxii Starbuck, Alexander, *History of the American whale fishery from its earliest inception to the year 1876.* Publisher: Waltham, Mass, The author, 1878, p.312

xxxiii Starbuck, Alexander, *History of the American whale fishery from its earliest inception to the year 1876.* Publisher: Waltham, Mass, The author, 1878, p.313

xxxiv Deed dated 3 May 1843, filed 25 March, 1863. Grantor: Esther Gad Williams; Grantee: Pyrrhus Gad. Copy in possession of Writer.

xxxv Ibid.

xxxvi Log 754; Logbook, 1849, 8 Feb-11May 1850, Sabina, p.3. Original scans & text transcript, online at www.mysticseaport.org/library/initiative/MsList.cfm.

xxxvii Ibid, pp. 4-5.

xxxviii Ibid, p.64.

xxxix Ibid, p.6.

xl Ibid, p.57.

xli Ancestry.com "New York Passenger Lists 1820-1950", microfilm M237-94.

xlii United States Population Census 1840, New York, Suffolk County, Southampton Town, p. 151, l.26, Household of Shadrach Consor, NARA Schedule M704-343.

xliii Transcript of Death Certificate for Pyrhus *(sic)* Concer *(sic)*, Index #72, District # 5126, date of death 8/23/1897, dated 3/11/2014. Repository: Registrar, Village of Southampton, 116 Hampton Road, Southampton, NY.

xliv Census 1850, New York, Suffolk County, Southampton Town, p. 371-B, l.16, Household of Pyrrhus Consor: p.355, l.50, Household of Shadrach Consor, NARA Schedule M432-602.

[xlv] Ibid. l.20, Household of Prince Williams.

[xlvi] Deed, dated 5 Apr 1854, filed 25 Mar 1863, Grantor: Sylvanus Howell, Grantee: Pyrrhus Conser (*sic*). Copy in possession of Writer.

[xlvii] Assessment Roll of the Town of Southampton for the year 1859. Copy in possession of Writer.

[xlviii] Census 1860, New York, Suffolk County, Southampton Town, p.593-B, l.20, Household of Pyrrhus Consor, NARA Schedule M653-865.

[xlix] Deed dated 15 Mar 1860, filed 25 March, 1860. Grantors: William and Abigail Jagger Grantee: Pyrrhus Concer. Copy in possession of Writer.

[ll] Assessment Roll of the Town of Southampton for the year 1865. Copy in possession of Writer.

[li] Census 1870, New York, Suffolk County, Southampton Town, p.198, l.30, Household of Pyrrhus Consor, NARA Schedule M593-1101.

[lii] Legal Notice re: Pyrrhus Conser (*sic*) –v- William F. Williams, his widow and heirs at large, Newspaper: Sag Harbor Express, dated 25 Jun 1891. Repository: www.fultonhistory.com. Online database.

[liii] Census 1880, New York, Suffolk County, Southampton Town, p.491, l.32, Household of Pyrrhus Consor, NARA Schedule T9935-1101.

[liv] New York, Suffolk, Southampton, Deaths 1881-1901, Southampton Town Clerk's Office, Reg. # 765, p.41. Record for Rachel A."Conser".

[lv] Register and Manual for the Use of Members of the Presbyterian Church of Southampton, L.I., Prepared February 1870, By Order of the Session, Published 1870, by Phair & Co., Book and Job Printers, 11 Frankfort St., New York; p.30.

[lvi] Probate of the Last Will and Testament of Temperance Williams. Will dated 15 November 1880, and proved 31 January 1882, at Surrogate's Court held at the house of William R. Post, in Southampton, Suffolk County, New York, before Surrogate Judge James H. Tuthill. Copy of proof (including Will) in possession of Writer.

[lvii] Deed of Sale, dated 18 May 1844, Grantor: Elizabeth Woolley, Grantee Temperance Williams, Town of Southampton, Suffolk County, New York. Copy in possession of Writer.

[lviii] See *supra*, note xxx.

[lix] Newspaper Article, Sag Harbor Express, The Pyrrhus Concer Will Case, 28 Apr 1898, Repository: www.fultonhistory.com, Online database.

CPSIA information can be obtained at www.ICGtesting.com
Printed in the USA
LVIW01n0700250418
574786LV00001B/4